G000243047

# WHEN
# *HARRY*
# MET
# *MEGHAN*

**hardie grant** books

When Harry Met Meghan

Published in 2018 by Hardie Grant Books,
an imprint of Hardie Grant Publishing

Hardie Grant Books (London)
5th & 6th Floors
52–54 Southwark Street
London SE1 1UN

Hardie Grant Books (Melbourne)
Building 1, 658 Church Street
Richmond, Victoria 3121

hardiegrantbooks.com

British Library Cataloguing-in-Publication Data. A catalogue
record for this book is available from the British Library.

ISBN: 978-1-78488-196-2

Publisher: Kate Pollard
Commissioning Editor: Kajal Mistry
Senior Editor: Molly Ahuja
Publishing Assistant: Eila Purvis
Design: Daisy Dudley
Illustrator: Michele Rosenthal
Images on pages 26, 27 © iStock
Images on pages 50, 70, 71 © Flat Icon

Colour Reproduction by p2d
Printed and bound in Slovenia by Gorenjski Tisk Storitve d.o.o.

# Contents

"**This beautiful woman literally** *TRIPPED...*

# AND FELL

## into my life."

"We had two dates
in London last July,
and it was I think
about three, maybe
four weeks later that
I managed to persuade
her to come and join
me in Botswana,
and we..."

# CAMPED OUT

### with each other

# UNDER THE STARS."

**"The fact that I fell in love with Meghan so incredibly quickly is confirmation to me that...**

# *ALL THE STARS* are *ALIGNED."*

**"I tried to warn [Meghan] as much as possible, but I think both of us were totally surprised by the reaction—after the first five or six months that we had to ourselves...**

I think you can have as many conversations as you want and try and prepare as much as possible, but we were totally unprepared for what happened after that."

# "The corgis took to [her] straight away...

I spent the last
33 years being barked
at; this one walks in—
absolutely nothing!"

[On what Princess Diana would think of Meghan]

"They'd be thick as thieves, without question. And she would be...

# *OVER THE MOON,* jumping up and down, *SO EXCITED FOR ME."*

**"It is days like today when I really miss having [my mum] around and being able to share the happy news...**

But with the ring and
with everything else
that's going on,
I'm sure that she's
with us."

# "WHEN DID I KNOW

### she was 'The One?'...

# The very
# *FIRST TIME WE MET.*"

[On their first meeting]
**"I was**

# *BEAUTIFULLY...*

# *SURPRISED*

## when I walked into that room and saw her."

"I know that at the end of the day, she chooses me. I choose her. Whatever we have to tackle will be done together as a team."

O N

H A R R Y

**[On the proposal]**

**❝It was just a cosy night. We were trying to roast a chicken. It was just an amazing surprise. It was so sweet and natural and very romantic. He got down on one knee...**

as a matter of fact,
I could barely let [him]
finish proposing, like,

*'CAN I
SAY YES
NOW?!'"*

**"I think I can very safely say, as naive as it sounds now, having gone through this learning curve in the past year and a half...**

I did not have any
understanding of
just what it would
be like."

**"It was definitely a set-up, it was a blind date. Because I'm from the States, you don't grow up with the same kind of understanding of the Royal family, I didn't know much about him...**

So the only thing that I had asked her [the mutual friend] was 'is he nice?' because if he wasn't kind, it didn't seem like we would make sense."

"There's a misconception that because I have worked in the entertainment industry that this was something I'd be familiar with. But, even though I'd been on my show for six years at that point and working before that...

I'd never been part
of tabloid culture;
I was never in
pop culture to
that degree."

"We were just hit so hard at the beginning with a lot of mistruths that I made the choice to not read anything, positive or negative...

It just didn't make sense, and instead we focused all of our energy just on nurturing our relationship."

[On personal attacks
in the press]
**"Of course it's
disheartening. It's a
shame that that is the
climate in this world,
to be discriminatory
in that sense...**

I think, you know,
at the end of the day,
I'm really just proud
of who I am and where
I've come from and
we have never put any
focus on that."

**[On Queen Elizabeth II]**

**"To be able to meet her through his lens, not just with his honour and respect for her as the monarch, but the love that he has for her as his grandmother...**

all of those layers have been so important for me, so that when I met her, I had such a deep understanding and, of course incredible respect for being able to have that time with her ... she's an incredible woman.**"**

[On the engagement ring]

"Everything about Harry's thoughtfulness and the inclusion of that, and obviously not being able to meet his Mum...

it's so important to
me to know that

# SHE'S
# A PART OF
# THIS
# WITH US."

"We were very quietly dating for about six months before it became news, and I was working during that whole time; the only thing that changed was people's perception...

Nothing about me changed. I'm still the same person, and I've never defined myself by my relationship."

# "WE'RE
## two people who are
# REALLY
# HAPPY
## and
# IN LOVE."

# HARRY

## ON

# LOVE &
# RELATIONSHIPS

# "I'VE LONGED FOR KIDS

## since I was very, very young...

I'm waiting to find the right person, someone who's willing to take on the job."

"**I'm**
*STILL*
*VERY MUCH*
*A KID*
*INSIDE*
**myself.**"

On mutual respect...

"*THIS IS NOT JUST ABOUT WOMEN...*

# Men need to recognise the part we play, too."

# "REAL MEN TREAT WOMEN...

with the

# *DIGNITY AND RESPECT*

they deserve."

# "[I'm in a rush]
# TO MAKE
# SOMETHING
# OF
# MY LIFE...

I feel there is just a
smallish window when
people are interested
in me before
[William's children]
take over, and
I've got to make the
most of it."

## "I am determined to have a relatively normal life...

and if I am lucky
enough to have
children, they can
have one too."

**"I sometimes still feel**

*I AM LIVING*

*IN A*

*GOLDFISH*

*BOWL...*

but I now manage
it better."

# "I STILL HAVE A NAUGHTY STREAK TOO...

which I enjoy, and it's
how I relate to those
individuals who
have got themselves
into trouble."

**"I don't think you can ever be urged to settle down. If you find the right person and everything feels right, then it takes time..."**

**especially for myself
and my brother."**

**"I'm not so much**
*SEARCHING*
*FOR*
*SOMEONE*
*TO FULFIL*
*THE ROLE...*

but obviously, you know, finding someone that would be willing to take it on."

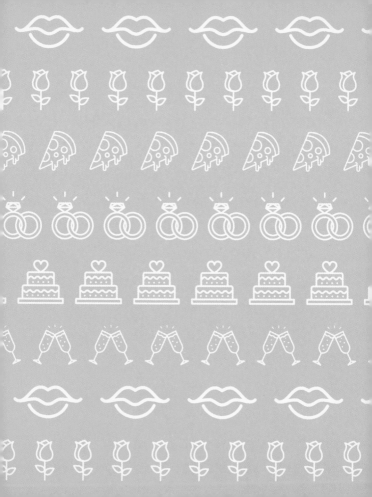

# MEGHAN

## ON

# LOVE

# &

# RELATIONSHIPS

"At the end of the day, if a guy is going to write a girl a letter, whether it's chicken scratch or scribble or looks like a doctor's note, if he takes the time to put pen to paper and not type it...

there's something
*SO*
*INCREDIBLY*
*ROMANTIC*
*AND*
*BEAUTIFUL*
about that."

# "I'm a sucker for a...

# *COMPLIMENT."*

**"I've had dates at the nicest restaurants, but when you leave, you're starving, and**

# *THE BEST PART OF THE DATE*

**is having...**

# *A SLICE OF PIZZA*

and a couple of drinks on the way home. I think it's important to be able to roll with the punches and enjoy every minute of it."

# "*I DREAM PRETTY BIG*,

## but truly had no idea my...

# *LIFE COULD BE THIS AWESOME..."*

# "I am the

# *LUCKIEST*
# *GIRL*
# *IN THE*
# *WORLD*,

## without question!"

**"It's really attractive if a man has a skill that you want to improve in yourself...**

If you can learn
from someone,
*THEN
THAT'S
SEXY."*

"I'm really big
on day dates. If you
go for a stroll,

*HAVE
A PICNIC*

or lunch with
a glass of wine...

# IT DOESN'T GET BETTER THAN THAT."

# "KINDNESS
### is the
## NO. 1
## QUALITY...

I look for in a man.
You can see it in how
he treats anyone –
from a **CEO** to a
housekeeper – and it's
a reflection of how
nice a guy is...

# Funniness and confidence come after that."

**"When a guy approaches me, it's fantastic if he can**

*MAKE ME LAUGH."*

**"It's all about balance; I have so much happiness in my career and am fortunate to travel the world and see so many amazing things...**

– it will also be nice to be anchored to something grounded. Raising a family will be a wonderful part of that.**"**

## "I love how British guys dress for the cold."

# "*CATTY IS NOT COOL...*

I can't think of anything less becoming than a man who talks about people behind their backs."

# SOURCES

*BBC*, 27th November 2017 – pp. **6-7, 8-9, 10-11, 12-13, 14-15, 16-17, 18-19, 22-23, 24, 28-29, 30-31, 32-33, 34-35, 36-37, 38-39, 40-41, 42-43**

*Daily Mail*, 1st November 2016 – pp. **54-55**

*Elle*, 13th November 2016 – pp. **52-53**

*Esquire*, 17th July 2013 – p. **50-51**

*Esquire*, 15th December 2016 – pp. **60-61, 62-63, 64-67, 70**

*Guardian*, 22nd June 2017 – pp. **88-91**

*Huffington Post*, 28th May 2015 – pp. **56-58**

*Huffington Post*, 18th April 2017 – pp. **68-69**

*Marie Claire*, 22nd January 2013 – pp. **92-93**

*Marie Claire*, 10th October 2016 – pp. **80-83**

*Mirror*, 20th May 2017 – pp. **72-73**

*Mirror*, 15th September 2014 – p. **79**

*Reuters*, 27th November 2017 – pp. **20-21**

*Sunday Express*, 30th May 2012 – pp. **76-77**

*Telegraph*, 14th March 2012 – pp. **94-95**

*Telegraph*, 21st June 2017 – p. **86-87**

*Vanity Fair*, 6th September 2017 – pp. **44-45, 46**

*Vogue*, 21st June 2017 – p. **84-85**